THE GREAT STRENGTH OF FRUITS AND VEGETABLES

BY

SHARON C. POWELL

Disclaimer

This book has been composed for data purposes as it were. Each work has been made to make this book as complete and precise as could really be expected. In any case, there might be botches in typography or content.

Additionally, this book gives data simply up to the distributing date. Along these lines, this book ought to be utilized as an aide - not as a definitive source. The motivation behind this book is to instruct. The creator and the distributor don't warrant that the data contained in this book is completely finished and will not be liable for any blunders or exclusions.

The creator and distributor will have neither obligation nor obligation to any individual or substance concerning any misfortune or harm caused or asserted to be caused straightforwardly or by implication by this book.

TABLE OF CONTENTS

CHAPTER 1

WHY VITAMINS AND MINERALS ARE THE ANSWER

So many of us wish we had more energy, better abs, and keen concentration. We hope we could rest better around evening, and wish it was somewhat more straightforward to awaken (those last two focuses are connected, incidentally!).

This has prompted the rise of various businesses, all worked around aiding us to feel, look, and perform better. We burn through gigantic measures of money on skincare items, rest supplements, and exercise center participation. We attempt a wide range of insane things, whether that is lying on a bed of delicate spikes to further develop rest (indeed, that is a genuine article!), wearing blue-obstructing conceals the entire day, or wearing energy-mending precious stones (which are similarly successful as wishing truly hard!).

We attempt these things since we're searching for replies, and we're frantic. We're willing to have a go at anything. Furthermore, we trust, each time, that we're going to coincidentally find the response and open our maximum capacity. We trust that ONE of these things will give the response and assist us with feeling GREAT as we realize that we truly can do. Yet, not very many of these systems make any recognizable contrast.

The issue? We're overcomplicating matters. Furthermore, this is to a great extent due to the tremendous measure of promotion that gets tossed at us consistently. In truth, getting to the next level of how you look and feel is exceptionally straightforward: it's about the nuts and bolts!

Consider what is probably going to be your ongoing way of life and your current eating regimen. Lift your hand assuming that any of these focuses concern you:

• You don't deal with your five fruits and vegetables a day

• You eat a lot of handled food sources and prepared feasts

• You go to the rec center 3 times each week or less - and aren't especially portable the remainder of the time

• You don't get sufficient rest

• You are in a condition of persistent pressure because of work, family, and monetary

pressures

• You spend a ton of your spare energy on the couch, watching kid's shows

• You spend over eight hours daily taking a gander at a PC screen, with a slouched back, gazing at a splendid screen

• You invest scarcely any energy outside

• You drink debased faucet water

• You inhale hurtful exhaust cloud-filled air

This is a somewhat disheartening picture, yet it's valid for The majority of us. We don't eat enough greens, we don't rest, we gorge on sweet food varieties, and we're worried constantly. Then, at that point, we can't help thinking about why we don't feel 100 percent! Regardless of whether you got the majority of these things right, our cutting-edge ways of life are only totally horrendous for our wellbeing. This is valid directly down to the way that the vast majority of us are excessively agreeable - we have turned "adjusted" to an agreeable, tamed way of life, and subsequently, our bodies have failed to remember how to manage pressure or trouble.

Take going outside for example. The greater part of us simply don't adequately do this, which implies that we aren't getting the significant boost of daylight, which makes a difference to urge the body to create vitamin D, which thus controls things like chemical creation, rest, state of mind, even craving! Without that significant info (called an "outer zeitgebers" in the logical writing) our body loses a portion of its normal musicality and certain cycles are interfered.

However, at that point, there's the colossal advantage of being vulnerable. Even when the sun isn't out, being outside assists with supporting testosterone levels, reinforces our invulnerable framework, and even works on our capacity to direct our internal heat level.

Is it any wonder we consistently feel "stodgy" when we never train this piece of our wellbeing? In any event, investing energy barefooted on the earth (which trains minuscule muscles in the foot), in any event, plunging into the water and pausing our breathing (which prepares our lungs and further develops our CO2 balance)… these are everything our bodies need. What's more, we aren't giving them that. What's more, our bodies are decaying greatly subsequently. Look at a wolf in nature as an overweight, ruined homegrown canine. Which is better?

YOU are that homegrown canine. In addition, a very upsetting way of life and absence of rest.

CHAPTER 2

AN INTRODUCTION TO VITAMINS

Before we go further, we should inspect all the more intently the particular advantages of leafy foods and vegetables. Also, the primary spot to begin is by checking the nutrient content. It might shock you to realize that nutrients were found less than 100 years ago. Until they were formally found, specialists realized that specific food sources made a difference with specific states of being, however they didn't see the reason why.

For instance, the British Navy conveyed a stockpile of limes as soon as 1975 because specialists had tracked down that eating a specific sum every day, or drinking the juice, prevented mariners from getting scurvy. Nonetheless, it was only after 1912 that Casimir Funk, working in the UK afterward in the USA thought of the expression "vitamines," which later became nutrients. The investigation of nutrients has advanced since that time, and while the majority of us know the names of the most widely recognized nutrients, we may not continuously comprehend what they do.

There are two kinds of nutrients. These are fat solvent nutrients and water dissolvable nutrients. Fat solvent nutrients are those nutrients that the body can store. This intends that on the off chance that you don't utilize each of the nutrients that you consume, they can be put away in the body for use when the body is needing them. The conspicuous benefit of fat solvent nutrients is that assuming your eating routine is for a brief time ailing in one of these nutrients, you are less inclined to experience a lack. The burden of these sorts of nutrients is that assuming you consume a lot of one of them, then your body can't flush out the excess and you could experience the ill effects of a vitamin glut.

Fat Soluble Vitamins

The most normally realized fat solvent nutrients are vitamin A, vitamin D, vitamin E and vitamin K.

Vitamin A assists with keeping the skin saturated, as well as guaranteeing that the bodily fluid films stay wet, graceful, and smooth. It likewise assists with keeping up with solid visual perception in low light, as well as keeping the conceptive framework sound and advancing sound bone development. Wellsprings of vitamin An incorporate entire milk, spread, eggs, and liver. A type of vitamin A, carotenoids are viewed in red, yellow, and dull green vegetables and natural products.

Vitamin D is fundamental for the body to ingest calcium. In this way, it is capable of solid teeth and bones, very much like calcium. Notwithstanding, both are required and cooperate. Vitamin D is frequently added to 'invigorated' food sources as fat spreads furthermore, cereals. It is otherwise called the daylight nutrient as the fundamental wellspring of nutrient D comes from daylight.

Vitamin E is liable for keeping up with sound muscles, sensory system, and conceptive framework. It is likewise an enemy of an oxidant. Being fat solvent, it is put away in the body and can assist with safeguarding body cells from the impacts of free revolutionaries, which be harming other body cells. Wellsprings of vitamin E incorporate entire grains, nuts, raw grain oil, and green verdant vegetables. Ingesting too many nutrients is believed to be hazardous.

Vitamin K is fundamentally liable for blood coagulation. Without it, each time you cut yourself you would be at risk of draining to death. This nutrient additionally makes kidney tissues and bone. Wellsprings of vitamin K incorporate liver, cheddar, oats, dim green verdant vegetables, and organic product. It is likewise made in the digestive organs by cordial microorganisms.

Water dissolvable nutrients can't be put away in the body. This truly intends that if you consume a lot of one of these nutrients, the sum that isn't utilized is discharged through pee. The upside of water dissolvable nutrients is that you are improbable to experience the ill effects of excess. The disservice of these nutrients is that you might have to take in bigger sums as they can't be put away.

Assuming your eating regimen is lacking in one of these nutrients, in any event, for a brief time frame, you might endure side effects of lack of nutrients subsequently, there is no backup supply put away in your body.

Water Soluble Vitamins

The most commonly realized water solvent nutrients are L-ascorbic acid and the whole gathering of B nutrients. L-ascorbic acid is otherwise called ascorbic corrosive. It assists with keeping up with the body's connective tissues, that is to say, the muscle, fat, and bone structure. It additionally assists with mending wounds by accelerating the creation of new cells, is an anti-oxidant, and assists the body with engrossing iron. One more capability of L-ascorbic acid is to safeguard the body's invulnerable framework empowering it to battle disease.

Wellsprings of L-ascorbic acid incorporate organic products, natural product juices, and vegetables. The B gathering of nutrients comprises B1 or thiamin, B2 or riboflavin, B3 or niacin, B6 or pyridoxine, and B12 or cyanocobalamin. This gathering of nutrients is basically worried about keeping the body working appropriately.

Vitamin B1 is fundamental in assisting the body with processing energy from fats, liquor, and carbs. Wellsprings of this nutrient are lean pork, crude cereals, seeds, and nuts.

B2 assists the body with utilizing and digesting sugars and proteins and keeps up with a sound hunger. Wellsprings of B2 incorporate fish, poultry, meat, milk, and eggs. Brewer's yeast is a decent wellspring of this nutrient, as are dim verdant vegetables.

B3 is fundamental for appropriate development and empowering oxygen to course through body tissues. It is likewise answerable for keeping a sound hunger. Wellsprings of vitamin B3 incorporate strengthened bread and oats and meat.

B6 is answerable for getting supplements and energy from the food we eat. It makes a difference forestall coronary illness by eliminating the overabundance of homocysteine from the blood. Sources of B6 incorporate soya beans, implies, nuts, eggs, entire grains, fish, sheep, port, chicken, and milk.

B12 assists with making sound red platelets. It additionally empowers the body to send messages between the body's nerve cells, empowering us to hear, move, think, and do typical regular exercises. It is made by microscopic organisms in the body's small digestive tract. This nutrient is added to numerous food varieties, including grains, and even though it is a water solvent nutrient, it tends to be put away in the liver. Wellsprings of B12 include poultry, fish, milk, meat, and eggs.

The most effective way of guaranteeing that you take in sufficient water solvent and fat dissolvable nutrients are to eat a fair eating regimen. Assuming you feel that you might be lacking in some nutrients, you ought to counsel a specialist for exhortation.

CHAPTER 3

AN INTRODUCTION TO MINERALS AND OTHER AMAZING NUTRIENTS IN FRUITS AND VEGETABLES

Though organic products are regularly loaded with nutrients, minerals will generally come more from our vegetables - however, depending on it, the two leafy foods are loaded with both. In this way, a decent inquiry, to begin with, maybe: what is the contrast between a nutrient and a mineral?

Though nutrients are natural and in this manner are ordinarily very unpredictable (they can be separated by any semblance of intensity, air, and corrosive), minerals are then again inorganic. As a matter of fact, a mineral can really be a metal or a stone - something you could never truly consider being a crucial structure block in what makes you. However, to be sure minerals are pivotal to the sound capability of the human body. Iron for instance, is a significant mineral that the body uses to make hemoglobin - the red platelets that move around the body conveying oxygen.

Without this cycle, giving energy to the body would be inconceivable for the innumerable urgent capabilities that go on - including breathing, processing, and that's only the tip of the iceberg. Ordinarily, minerals will generally have a somewhat more basic job in the underlying components of the human body - and the harder components. For the model, minerals structure bones, ligaments, and tendons.

Minerals likewise assume a part in conduction, in any case. The body is fueled by power all things considered, and keeping up with the right charge is urgent for the sound capability of our muscles and cerebrum. That is the reason an erroneous equilibrium between sodium and potassium can cause squeezing, as the body can't send messages accurately to the muscles. In like manner, an absence of calcium can diminish strength as dealing with the charge in the muscle is required.

Are you aware? You can differentiate between an organic product furthermore, a vegetable in view of the seed/stone. Vegetables don't actually have them! Food varieties that have astounding orders include tomatoes (organic product), coconut (natural product), avocado (organic product), and cucumber(fruit).

Other Essential Micronutrients

As well as being plentiful in nutrients and minerals, products of the soil are likewise a rich wellspring of the two other fundamental supplements. The other fundamental supplements are fundamental unsaturated fats and fundamental amino acids. The expression "fundamental" implies that these substances can't be incorporated inside the body, thus in this way should be acquired from our eating regimen. Perhaps this maybe a piece of information regarding how enormous an issue it is that the vast majority of us are not getting them that way!

Anyway, what do these supplements do?

Indeed, amino acids are basically the structure blocks of proteins. We get a ton of these from meat, and our bodies will then, at that point, separate those constituent parts in a request to revamp our tissue. As we saw toward the beginning of this book, we in a real sense are what we eat! Therefore amino acids and proteins likewise are so significant for weight lifters and competitors attempting to construct muscle.

Research recommends that the ideal equilibrium for competitors is 1 gram of protein for each 1lb of bodyweight. Protein likewise has different advantages - it is a lot harder to convert into fat for example, and it has a thermogenic impact implying that just processing it will really consume calories! Hence, many individuals will be working diligently attempting to track down wellsprings of protein from meat and will eat a lot of chicken to fabricate greater muscles. This can turn out to be difficult work! In any case, what they neglect is that vegetables and even natural products too contain protein (however vegetables are marginally predominant in this sense). Try not to simply count the protein you got from that protein shake and chicken, think about how much is in the broccoli on the chicken.

Amino acids likewise play a large group of different jobs in the body and are utilized to deliver stomach-related catalysts, synapses (cerebrum synthetic substances), and considerably more. They can additionally do things, for example, making. At last, products of the soil contain fundamental unsaturated fats. These are significant fats that assist us with bettering retain different products of the soil, and furthermore serve asa scope of extra valuable advantages -, for example, upgrading mind capability (the cerebrum is made of a lot of fat!).

Omega 3 is quite possibly of the most remarkable fundamental unsaturated fat there is and has a Enormous host of astounding advantages. Frequently, we consider omega 3 to be something we get from fish. However, it likewise exists in great sums in kelp, hemp seed, pecans, kidney beans,and soybean.

CHAPTER 4:

FRUITS AND VEGETABLES FOR ATHLETIC PERFORMANCE

At the point when you consider an eating routine for building muscle, your brain likely goes to the exemplary choices. You probably will zero in fundamentally on protein sources like chicken, fish, and eggs. A competitor's eating routine ought to comprise only meat and steamed rice, isn't that so?

However, this is a long way from the main sort of food that will be valuable for constructing muscle and further developing execution. For lifting weights, running, truth be told, swimming, significant distance running, and some other sort of athletic pursuit it is exceptionally vital that you get a decent eating routine that will consolidate an extensive variety of different nutritional categories. Specifically, it is pivotal you get your fruits and vegetables.

Keen on taking enhancements to support your athletic exhibition? What could intrigue you to learn is that consuming leafy foods can really be more powerful while likewise costing substantially less and having a heap of other astounding medical advantages!

Here are a few models.

Top Fruits and Vegetables That Improve Athletic Performance

Beets

Beets are by a long shot among the extremely most significant vegetables for building muscle and for competitors, everything being equal. That is on the grounds that beets are among the best food sources on the planet when it comes to raising nitric oxide. Nitric oxide is a characteristic 'vasodilator'. This implies that it can cause the veins (veins and courses) to enlarge (extend) accordingly empowering the progression of oxygen and supplements around the body.

The outcome is that the muscles get more oxygen and energy during preparation and more supplements for improving recuperation. This can assist you with lifting for additional reps,running further distances, and recuperating at a quicker rate.

Potatoes

Starches are frequently described as miscreants yet truth be told they are very significant for building muscle and for actual preparation overall. Potatoes are a great decision for starch since they're likewise high in fiber, high in L-ascorbic acid (which improves recuperation), and low in calories. Consume after an exercise and the energy will go directly to the muscles as opposed to the midsection.

Spinach

Spinach is a vegetable that is high in protein as well, similar to a decent wellspring of phytoecdysteroids. These share nothing for all intents and purposes with anabolic steroids in any case, they might make a comparable difference - for certain investigations proposing they are a decent choice for empowering muscle building and testosterone creation.

Kale

Kale is the vegetable most noteworthy in calcium. Calcium is quite significant for your exercises, besides the fact that it assists with fortifying the bones yet it additionally builds up your connective tissue and it assists with reinforcing constrictions for a more touchy power during exercises. Kale is exceptionally popular right presently being high in protein and low in calories. A disgrace however, costs a fair piece!

Mushrooms

Mushrooms are in fact not natural products or vegetables, but rather they are seen as in the same passageway and they're ok for veggie lovers, so they're fair game to incorporate here. Mushrooms are one more incredible wellspring of protein as well as accompanied by an extensive variety of extra medical advantages and benefits. They're loaded with minerals, they can support recuperation from preparing and significantly more next to! It's inevitable until we begin seeing mushroom protein shakes springing up in wellbeing stores! The other astonishing advantage of mushrooms is that they contain vitamin D, they're one of a handful of the dietary wellsprings of vitamin D! (Another being slick fish).

This is significant seeing as vitamin D is viewed as an expert chemical controller, and is answerable for empowering the creation of testosterone in specific - one of the vitally anabolic chemicals for building muscle and consuming fat. In addition, vitamin D has as of late been demonstrated to be substantially more powerful than even L-ascorbic acid with regards to supporting the invulnerable framework and forestalling colds and illnesses. As any competitor knows, a virus can be sufficient to complete a wreck and competitors prepare a plan, which thus can be the distinction between triumph and disappointment!

Carrots

Carrots are for the most part sound and an incredible wellspring of vitamin A, C, and K. What's truly intriguing about them however is the lutein, which might assist with expanding energy levels and upgrade the proficiency of your very mitochondria! Your mitochondria are the energy manufacturing plants of your phones which convert glucose into ATP (glucose being the sugar that comes from carbs, and ATP is the usable type of energy in your body). This in short means that with carrots and different wellsprings of lutein, you can really run quicker and that you'll truly consume more calories in any event, while you're resting!

In one review, rodents were given lutein (which needs a wellspring of fat to retain, for example, milk) and it was found that they started running significant distances deliberately in their wheel, consuming considerably more fat as they did

Apples

Apples are plentiful in L-ascorbic acid, which is one more pivotal nutrient for improving the invulnerable framework and assisting competitors with preparing longer and harder as a general rule. L-ascorbic acid additionally assists with empowering the maintenance of muscle tissue, increments serotonin to help with mental recuperation, and even build the development of both testosterone and nitric oxide when matched with zinc.

On top of this, apples are likewise extremely wealthy in fiber, which can assist with moving along solid discharges, the ingestion of food, and pulse, and that's only the tip of the iceberg.

Fiber is likewise key to supporting a solid microbiome, which thus can uphold a sound safe framework, better mindset, weight reduction, and considerably more.

CHAPTER 5:

ASTOUNDING SUPERFOOD FRUITS AND VEGETABLES FOR MOOD, ENERGY, BEAUTY AND MORE

Anyway, you're not especially intrigued by weight reduction? Maybe you are now content with the size you are. (Bravo!)

Perhaps you're not a competitor? Perhaps you don't have observable wellbeing issues?

See, fruits and vegetables are for everybody. Also, just to smash that point home, here are a few additional instances of fruits and vegetables with stunningly shifting different sound advantages.

Broccoli and Leafy Greens for Beauty and Pregnancy

Indeed, fruits and vegetables can assist with making you look more gorgeous. Furthermore, that is genuine even of something as basic as your unassuming broccoli! Broccoli is maybe somewhat less 'intriguing' when contrasted and a portion of the other superfood fruits and vegetables on this rundown. However, don't let that fool you: this is still an extraordinarily nutritious food that everybody ought to get a greater amount of.

Once more, first of all, broccoli is a decent wellspring of fiber and can assist with getting to the next level of your assimilation, your solid discharges, and significantly more. However, broccoli is likewise extremely high in nutrients K, L-ascorbic acid, fiber, potassium, collagen, iron, and calcium.

How about we start by jumping into that collagen? This is the sort of thing that we all need yet not very many of us get it. Collagen has been displayed to further develop mind capability and battle against Alzheimer's, it additionally assists with decreasing back torment, further develops skin flexibility, reinforces the nails, battles flawed stomach disorder, battles knee torment. It also strengthens your ligaments, tendons, and bones. Therefore feasts, for example, bone stock is amazingly great for us. Presently, later research is proposing a considerably more remarkable explanation that collagen may be so significant.

Scientists currently suspect that people would have lived principally by eating bone marrow from creature corpses. The contention goes that tracker finders might have been unprepared to take on enormous prey. Nonetheless, we were truly adept at finding our prey and following them. What probably would have happened frequently, is that we would have followed gazelles and different creatures to the place where they were gone after and killed by creatures like lions and tigers. They would then have stripped those creatures of all their meat, abandoning the skeleton. That is the point at which the shrewdness and clever people would have gone along, torn open the bones with our material hands, and afterward eaten the nutritious collagen from inside.

In the event that this is for sure obvious, we advanced in a climate where we consumed a lot of the constituents of bone. What's more, we presently end up flung into a world where we seldom get these essential supplements. On the off chance that that is the situation, broccoli might be much more useful than we at first expected!

Pregnant moms ought to investigate eating more broccoli that is, on the grounds that both broccoli and numerous plates of mixed green leaves are a decent wellspring of folate, which is something that all moms are prescribed to eat. Not getting sufficient folate expands the gamble of complexities in pregnancy, and that is the reason a lot of moms will attempt to get all the more falsely using pregnancy supplements.

This is where it means a lot to bring up the critical benefits of getting a larger number of supplements from your eating routine instead of from supplements. While the facts really confirm that you can profit from supplements, the education here is the name. These are expected to enhance your normal eating regimen. In other words that they ought to be taken notwithstanding your standard eating routine, rather than as another option. Supplements from your eating routine are definitely more powerful than those taken in pill structure, as they are joined with various different supplements, fats, strands, and different components.

Together, these assist in further developing ingestion of the vital components and that makes them significantly more viable. What to perceive is that the human body developed while being presented with these food varieties and hence is ideally planned to separate the dietary benefit here. Consuming supplements in an engineered form isn't planned. This is the reason so many tell you not to take nutrient tablets while starving'. They simply work better as food varieties.

Cayenne Pepper for Weight Loss, Testosterone, and More

Cayenne pepper in the meantime is one more extraordinary apparatus in the fight against irritation. This is a compound that makes food fiery and is broadly seen in balms and creams because of its enemy of irritation impacts. It's a typical aggravation help too as it drains nerve cells of the compound 'substance P'. Substance P causes both irritation and the vibe of torment, so this is something extraordinary to add to your eating regimen in the event that you really do experience the ill effects of a condition like fibromyalgia or joint pain.

Cayenne additionally comes loaded with flavonoids and carotenoids. These are cancer prevention agents that forestall cell harm, accordingly further fighting against aggravation. Cayenne pepper likewise has various other amazing advantages. It has been demonstrated to be a viable hunger suppressant, for example, intending that if you are somebody who battles to adhere to an eating regimen, you could begin tracking down it a bit simpler to be focused and in this way ideally see the weight start to tumble off.

Simultaneously, cayenne pepper might assist with further developing processing. This is significant on the grounds that better assimilation doesn't just give you more energy and forestall inconvenience, yet it additionally assists you with bettering assimilating supplements from your food. That implies that every one of the advantages you're getting from the other superfoods on this rundown will then be gone up to 11.

What's more, is that cayenne pepper has likewise been displayed to increment testosterone. This obviously is the chemical that the vast majority of us know as the 'male chemical' and is answerable for the male sex drive, as well as a large number of the contrasts among people.

Expanding testosterone in men increases muscle tone, lessens fat capacity, raises hostility, helps with recuperation, and strengthens the safe framework and that's just the beginning. Men who don't get sufficient testosterone will show indications of sorrow, low energy, low temperament, and low sex drive. They additionally battle with weight gain and low bulk. On the other hand, men with high testosterone display the characteristics that we partner with the exemplary 'extremely confident man' alongside conditioned and strong bodies.

This is the reason such countless men attempt to increase their regular testosterone creation using steroids and different medications - notwithstanding those conveying various wellbeing alerts and serious risks. The truly stressing part is that testosterone in men is expanding across the globe by 1% every year. This is halfway because of the utilization of ladylike items and their effect on our water, alongside a large group of different issues (certain plastics and our for the most part dormant ways of life). Be that as it may, the diet has a BIG impact on it as well. Time to begin eating somewhat less handled food, and somewhat more cayenne pepper.

Elderberry for Inflammation

Elderberry is a berry that is wealthy in supplements. Once more an organic product is missing from a significant number of our ordinary eating regimens, as it's one that you ought to consider once again introducing. The basic truth is that the majority of us depend on similar products of the soil vegetables every day of the week. Along these lines, however, we are guaranteeing we get a lot of supplements basically while passing up some others. The best eating regimen is the most shifted diet - the one that incorporates the greatest scope of various natural products, vegetables, meats, and spices, from there, the sky is the limit.

So how could elderberry at any point help you?

Elderberry has been utilized since ancient times and has been utilized as a supplement or medication by a large group of old societies - including the Ancient Egyptians. Today we currently realize that these organic products are unquestionably high in flavonoids, what's more, particularly our companion's anthocyanins - strong cell reinforcements like resveratrol. Simultaneously, elderberries have been displayed to help boost the creation of cytokines. These are the courier particles that our bodies use to control the resistant framework. Expert incendiary cytokines help to energize aggravation, while calming cytokines help to diminish them. This is all vital on the grounds that it essentially guarantees that the body can appropriately manage its own reaction to infections and sicknesses, and assist with recuperating wounds and wounds.

However, a considerable lot of us believe that irritation is consistently something terrible - as a matter of fact, irritation assists with obliterating diseases before they get an opportunity to produce results, as well as to support recuperating by conveying more supplements to the impacted region. The issue is the point at which this reaction goes haywire. It would seem for comparative reasons, elderberry could likewise be exceptionally powerful at fighting sensitivities!

On top of this, elderberries are likewise exceptionally successful at fighting and obliterating microorganisms, being valuable in battling contaminations, colds, and a large group of different issues. Generally fascinating of all, the little berries contain powerful antiviral specialists that have been displayed to really 'deactivate' infections. These work by forestalling the infections from having the option to get through cell walls utilizing their haemagglutinin spikes, which thusly delivers them practically dormant. They are consequently exceptionally powerful for battling issues like rhinitis, as well as forestalling them from happening in any case.

Obviously, there is additionally the standard nutrient and mineral substance that you tend to get from berries.

CHAPTER 6:

HOW ANTIOXIDANTS ASSIST YOU WITH LIVING LONGER

Cell reinforcements are tracked down normally in our eating regimen and are likewise a critical component of numerous enhancements. Cell reinforcements are something of a trendy expression nowadays and cell reinforcement nutrients and minerals as well as a scope of Naka Herb supplements are profoundly famous.

What is the justification for this? Also, what definitively are cancer prevention agents? Here we will look a little at how cell functions, how a cell bites the dust, and why cancer prevention agents are so significant.

Our cells are comprised of different parts however all you want to be familiar with in this example is the cell wall and the core. The cell wall, encompassed by mitochondria, is the piece of the cell that keeps it all intact and gives the cell its round appearance.

In the interim, the core is the focal point of the cell, which is frequently alluded to as the 'control focus'. Here is where the DNA is put away, the 'plan' that tells the cell what it resembles, how to act, and where the other significant cells go in the body. However, what's likewise in our body is 'free revolutionaries' and this is where the cancer prevention agent nutrients and minerals and the Naka Herb supplements come in.

Basically, free revolutionaries are substances that move around the body and harm the cells. They are a side-effect of numerous things from essentially breathing (oxygen is receptive and harms cells) to getting an excessive amount of direct daylight (the UV waves in the daylight are radioactive and can harm our cell walls as well). These free extremists then cause a great deal of serious harm to the body and are sufficient to in the long run make our skin look more seasoned - because the harm however minuscule can ultimately amount to be noticeable to the unaided eye and this goes for skin cells as well. For this reason, bunches of openness to the sun will do right by you, and tanned in the present moment, at the end of the day bring about your skin seeming badly creased and weathered.

All the more genuinely, however, ultimately these free revolutionaries will break as far as possible through the cell walls, and this will imply that they arrive at the core where the DNA is housed. On the off chance that they arrive at this, they can make harm your hereditary code, and this outcome in the transformation changes the outflow of the cell and renders it unfit to take care of its business.

Since cells duplicate by parting (mitosis) this then, at that point, implies that when the cell parts it will duplicate the DNA across and you will have two issue cells. Your safe framework attempts to stop this and can be supported on the off chance that you purchase spices on the web, however, it would be better obviously if it very well may be forestalled. Those dead cells as they spread become a disease, and can ultimately prompt the disappointment of entire organs. Cell reinforcement nutrients and minerals from organic products, vegetables, and even enhancements will assist you with doing this - by annihilating the free revolutionaries on influence accordingly forestalling them truly causing that harm. These will then, at that point, slow your noticeable maturing and assist with stopping malignant growth - not terrible!

CHAPTER 7

STEP-BY-STEP INSTRUCTIONS ON THE USE OF FRUITS AND VEGETABLES TO SUCCESSFULLY IMPROVE YOUR HEALTH

As of now, you ought to have an exhaustive thought of the best motivations to guarantee you are getting an adequate number of leafy foods in your eating regimen. These can upgrade your wellbeing in a bunch of ways, and on the off chance that you are as of now feeling drained, ill-humored, unwell, or indeed, even discouraged, almost certainly, you have a lack in no less than one of these micronutrients. What's more, this ought to shock no one - considering that by far most individuals DO have a lack these days of some sort or another.

The following inquiry is how you ought to be delicately coordinating these leafy foods and vegetables. Are there any disadvantages? What number do you want definitively? Can you simply utilize a nutrient tablet all things considered?

The Number of Fruits and Vegetables That You Need Really?
You could have heard that you ought to mean to consume no less than five various products of the soil a day. This is a piece of general counsel that is given by numerous wellbeing associations and state-run administrations. A few associations have expanded this number to seven. It is a word of wisdom, but it is likewise erratic.

What do I mean by that? Basically, that depends on nothing!
Products of the soil are not intrinsically great for you. They are not great for you since they are foods grown from the ground. Rather, they are great for you BECAUSE they contain that multitude of fundamental micronutrients. Those micronutrients are expected in various amounts and assortments, and eventually, the smartest course of action for our wellbeing is simply to get an as considerable lot of them as could be expected. The more products of the soil you consume, the better. Also, it is exceptionally difficult to go too far when you get your supplements from normal sources like this.

Furthermore, be exceptionally questionable when a bundle of food lets you know it considers "one of your five a day." If that food is profoundly handled, then, at that point, odds are it will not contain quite a large number of supplements in it by any stretch of the imagination any longer. In any event, it is probably going to be a lot lower in fiber.

Subsequently, the advantages will not be just about as incredible as they would have been had you consumed that supplement itself. Apply some presence of mind, and where conceivable, eat as a large number of entire, genuine organic products and vegetables as you can!

The Dangers of Too Many Fruits and Vegetables
All things considered, you can cause yourself harm by consuming an excessive number of leafy foods and vegetables. Or on the other hand, to be somewhat more unambiguous, it is generally simple to hurt by consuming an excessive amount of organic products. That is because the organic product is exceptionally acidic and loaded with sugar. Both these things make it harmful to your teeth specifically. Many individuals who change to eat fewer carbs that are focused on the utilization of smoothies will wind up creating serious tooth issues!

One answer for this is to try not to drink an excess of natural product juice or too many natural product smoothies. All things considered, center around drinking vegetable smoothies, which regularly contain much less sugar. Another thought is that products of the soil are as yet a wellspring of calories. This is particularly valid for things like avocados, which have turned into extremely popular as of late. While avocados are perfect for supporting testosterone (on account of their solid immersed fat substance), and keeping in mind that they are valuable for those attempting to stay away from carbs, they can in any case make you fat!

Try not to tragically imagine that "products of the soil are sound and subsequently can't make you fat." They contain calories you need to follow and deal with those calories to keep away from undesirable weight gain.

CHAPTER 8

MAKING A DIET RICH IN FRUITS AND VEGETABLES

In this way, you should eat more foods grown from the ground, and we've seen as of now that there are countless explicit food sources that have an especially great benefit - similarly as there are a colossal number of explicit nutrients and minerals thatyou really want to attempt to search out your eating regimen.

In any case, how would you approach carrying out that arrangement? How would you go from battling to get your five every day, to have the option to effortlessly consume enormous plenty of various gainful fixings?

Since that is the other key thing to understand: you ought not to be taking a reductive methodology of attempting to separately search out everything. Assuming you do this, then, at that point, you'll find that you wind up burning through a gigantic measure of cash, and eventually not getting a lot of advantage.

This book has recorded an immense number of leafy foods that you can search out explicitly to appreciate benefits for your excellence, for your energy levels, irritation, insusceptibility... You could accordingly be enticed to figure you can single out the advantages you need! Yet, this is an unacceptable methodology. At the point when there is a wide range of superfoods that each proposition has some sort of astounding advantage, you can't search out every one independently. This is particularly evident considering to be large numbers of them won't combine as one, many aren't accessible in your neighborhood store, and some may be palatable for a short measure of time. Anyway, what do you do all things being equal?

The Strategy: The Aim is Variety

Rather than searching out individual various leafy foods, what is far ideal is just mean to get the greatest assortment you can in your diet. By doing this, you will cover the biggest range of fixings, and consequently, get the biggest scope of various advantages from your eating regimen.

You could find the best superfood vegetable on the planet, however assuming that was all you ate then you wouldn't get all that much advantage - on the grounds that you'd just be getting a lot of those equivalent fixings.

We don't consider food sources, for example, apples as being super food sources, but since they contain a lot of L-ascorbic acids (cell reinforcement, supports testosterone, energizes nitric oxide arrangement, produces serotonin), epicatechin, they are similarly as noteworthy as those more intriguing thoughts. Also, on the off chance that you eat three distinct leafy foods, the scope of supplements you get will be far more noteworthy.

Studies shows, that our microbiome - the sound microscopic organisms living in our guts - benefit in particular from a fluctuated diet. The more prominent the scope of food sources you eat, the more grounded your stomach wellbeing will be - bringing about weight reduction, more energy, and a better mindset, from there, the sky is the limit.

At long last, by intending to simply "eat heaps of foods grown from the ground" you can decrease the measure of thought this diet support includes, which thusly will assist you with being more liable to adhere to your new responsibility.

The Most Effective Method To Increase The Variety of Fruits and Vegetables
So how would you expand the assortment? Here are a few simple tips that will assist you with doing that without adding a ton of stress to your next shopping trip:

• Make loads of stews, hot pots, and Italian dishes. Assuming you're cooking something like a bolognaise, then, at that point, it's entirely simple to toss a bundle of fruits and vegetables into a pot with some mince.

• To make this significantly more straightforward, take a stab at grinding things like carrot (so you needn't bother with to strip), and use frozen ingredients like mushrooms, peas, and sweetcorn.

• Make loads of servings of mixed greens! A simple method for making a virus lunch is to get a plate of mixed greens leaves, toss on some sweet potatoes, slice some cucumber, and add a spot of lemon. This can go on almost ANYTHING you cook. Pick child leaf spinach and you'll get iron and folate. Then differ which leaf you utilize without fail.

• Hold up! While doing this, concoct enormous groups of food varieties and afterward freeze them in heaps of separately partitioned Tupperware. Then, at that point, all you want to do is to thaw out everyone as you come to eat it.

• Make smoothies! These are very simple to create - toss a pack of products of the soil/vegetables in and hit mix. They likewise give a colossal increase in astounding advantages. The absolute generally vigorous and blissful individuals I know consume everyday smoothies.

• Purchase leafy foods out. A lot of bistros sell natural products at the counter, and the equivalent is valid in numerous merchants. Rather than purchasing a chocolatey nibble, simply purchase the most fascinating-looking organic product you can find.

CHAPTER 9

MULTIVITAMIN SUPPLEMENTS

Assuming that the principal advantages of leafy foods come from the nutrients, minerals and other fundamental micronutrients, then, at that point, you could have a truly sensible question: shouldn't something be said about multivitamins?

A multivitamin supplement is an enhancement that contains an equilibrium of various supplements. You could commonly see one that contains a mix of L-ascorbic acid, D, A, and B complex. Similarly, multimineral enhancements may contain Iron, Magnesium, Potassium, Calcium, and Zinc for "sound bones also, chemical equilibrium."

Are these items comparably great as the "genuine article?" Indeed and negative.
From one perspective, you can assimilate and profit from supplements. Certain individuals will let you know that this isn't correct, yet there are a few valid justifications to accept in any case. As far as one might be concerned, did you have at least some idea that there really exist a few items that are intended to supplant your whole eating routine? These incorporate any semblance of Soylent, which as far as anyone knows contains each and every supplement the body needs, all reasonably impeccably.

Is it a smart thought? Not by any stretch! However, what to zero in on right presently is that individuals who utilize this item get by... and they're quite sound! Also, with that in mind, we can in this way state without a doubt that multivitamins can likewise be retained, Be that as it may, there's a trick. The first of these gets is that a multivitamin is just going to be pretty much as great as the individual who planned it. We saw with lutein and other fat- dissolvable nutrients for instance. These need a wellspring of fat to be consumed into the circulation system. Get them from normal food sources, and odds are the wellspring of fat will be incorporated. Get them from a nutrient enhancement and they might not.

Comparative associations additionally exist between numerous different nutrients and minerals, where one will help the other to handily be retained more. In like manner, unique nutrients and minerals assimilate at various rates, thus preferably shouldn't be joined into a solitary item. Then there are different things that leafy foods contain that do us great - like fiber, and amino acids, from there, the sky is the limit. Also, there's the little truth that all fruits and vegetables contain substances that we don't completely have any idea about or maybe aren't even mindful of.

We just barely found the exceptional advantages of lutein (that go past eye wellbeing). So eating genuine fruits and vegetables is ALWAYS best. Yet, so, in the event that the decision comes down to utilizing an enhancement or not getting those advantageous supplements by any means... then the enhancement is obviously better. an enhancement can be an exceptionally helpful and simple method for getting what you want in your eating regimen, or can be viewed as a "backup."

CONCLUSION

YOUR OUTLINE FOR GREATER HEALTH

What's more, with that, we arrive at the finish of this aide. Right now, you ought to now have a greatly improved thought of definitively which foods are grown from the ground you want in your eating regimen, which ones can give the most advantages, and how the assortment of these things beat all the other things. In like manner, you ought to now have a comprehension of the most effective ways to get those leafy foods in your eating routine, and the most ideal ways to keep away from any issues that can come from them.

With everything that is expressed, here is your diagram to help your well-being and joy enormously by getting more leafy foods:

• Begin your day with a smoothie, however, don't have more than one natural product smoothie

• Try not to mean to get only 5-7 fruits and vegetables in your eating regimen. Get as a large number as you can to get a fluctuated blend.

• Utilize an enhancement as a "backup." This is likewise particularly helpful when searching out more dark and rare nutrients.

• In any case, ensure that you read the directions and do your examination. You might wish to think about timing and adding a wellspring of fat to help retention.

• Use methodologies to make it as simple as conceivable to get more products of the soil vegetables in your eating routine

• Keep away from handled food varieties and "void calories" - supplant things like chips and chocolate bars with plates of mixed greens and carrot sticks

• Keep up with this program for 30 days. You ought to find you notice you have more energy, drive, and better health.

• Utilize this new energy to work on your way of life in alternate ways!